4. Arpeggio can-can

Jacques Offenbach (1819–80)
arr. KB & DB

5. Wake up! (round and ostinato)

KB & DB

f Wake up in the morn - in', ev -'ry-one's still snor - in',
p Sleep - y in the eve - nin', soon we will be dream - in',

get 'em out of bed with a wake up shout. Hey!
time to go to bed with a lul - la - by. Shh!

New parts enter at ✳. The last two bars can also be played as an ostinato.

1. Show time!

KB & DB

Lively ♩ = 112

✳ Either or both of these parts may be played.

2. Sword dance

Thoinot Arbeau (1520–95)
arr. KB & DB

Majestic ♩ = 112

3. Let's play a rag

KB & DB

Not too fast ♩ = 116

Double Bass

String Time Starters

21 pieces for flexible ensemble

Kathy and David Blackwell

Illustrations by Martin Remphry

Full performances and backing tracks for all pieces are available to download from the *String Time Starters* Companion Website: www.oup.co.uk/companion/stringtimestarters.

MUSIC DEPARTMENT

OXFORD
UNIVERSITY PRESS

Just for Starters: warm ups

1. Hill and gully rider

Jamaican trad.
arr. KB & DB

2. Aiken drum

Scottish trad.
arr. KB & DB

3. Pizzicato polka

Johann Strauss II (1825–99)
arr. KB & DB

Printed in Great Britain
OXFORD UNIVERSITY PRESS, MUSIC DEPARTMENT, GREAT CLARENDON STREET, OXFORD OX2 6DP

4. Midnight feast

KB & DB

Tip - toe, tip - toe, tip - toe, tip - toe. Yum!

5. Chicken on a fencepost

American trad.
arr. KB & DB

6. Mellow-D

KB & DB

7. Take your partners

KB & DB

8. Daydream

Gently ♩ = 108

KB & DB

9. Take the D train

1st time: Slow ♩ = 92; 2nd time: Fast! ♩ = 116

KB & DB

* pizz. or arco

* pizz. or arco

1st time: gradually get faster

* Either or both parts may be played.

Give the effect of a train gradually gathering speed then travelling at a fast pace.

10. Three-legged race

KB & DB

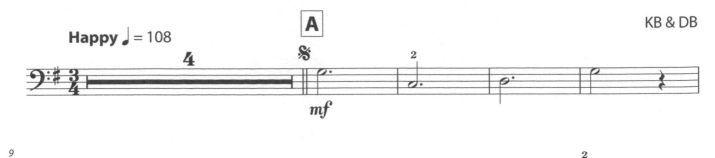

11. Boogie

KB & DB

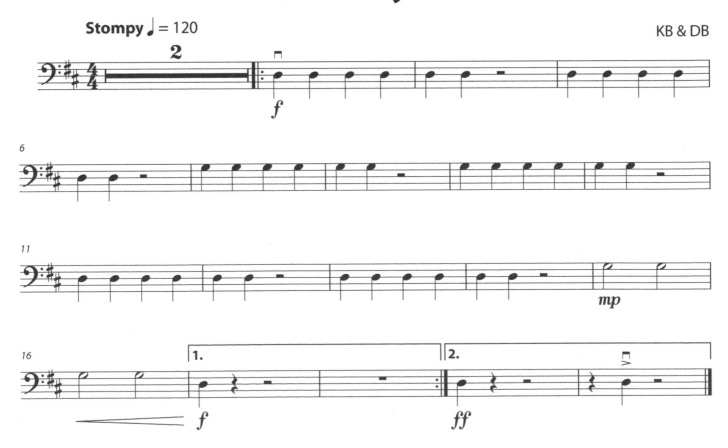

12. Time to tango

KB & DB

13. Let's rock!

14. Circus tricks

Lively ♩ = 132

KB & DB

15. Ode to Joy

Ludwig van Beethoven (1770–1827)
arr. KB & DB

Joyfully ♩ = 100

16. Skye boat song

Scottish trad.
arr. KB & DB

Gently flowing ♩ = 100

A

B

C

rall.

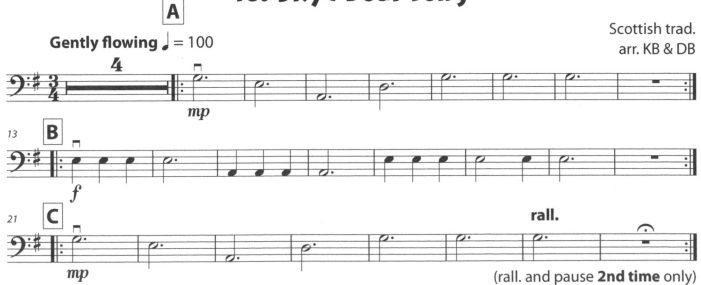

(rall. and pause **2nd time** only)

17. Mary had a baby

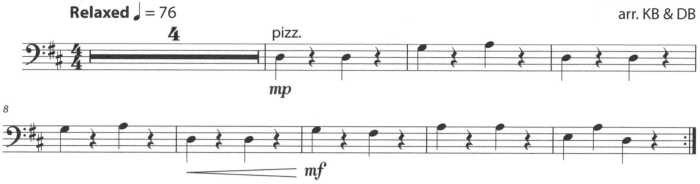

American trad.
arr. KB & DB

18. Jingle, bells

J. Pierpont (1822–93)
arr. KB & DB

19. Canoe song

Native American Indian song
arr. KB & DB

20. G-force blues

KB & DB

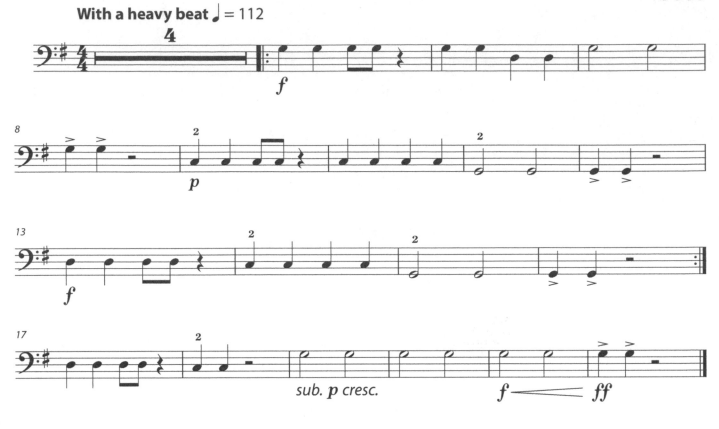

With a heavy beat ♩ = 112

21. Hush, little baby

American trad.
arr. KB & DB

repeat ad lib.

Gently flowing ♩ = 72

pizz.

rall.　　, Slower

ISBN 978-0-19-341161-6